Reading Rousers
114 WAYS TO READING FUN

MARIAN R. BARTCH
JERRY J. MALLETT

Goodyear Publishing Company, Inc.
Santa Monica, California 90401

To Jerry Rottier,
for his constant friendship and encouragement.

Copyright © 1980
Goodyear Publishing Company, Inc.
Santa Monica, California 90401

Y-7595-5

Current printing (last digit)
10 9 8 7 6 5 4 3 2 1

Printed in the United States of America

Library of Congress Cataloging in Publication Data

Bartch, Marian R.
   Reading rousers.
   1. Individualized reading instruction.
2. Children — Books and reading. 3. Motivation in
education. I. Mallett, Jerry J., 1939-   joint
author. II. Title.
LB1050.38.B38   372.4'147   80-20284
ISBN 0-8302-7595-9

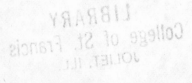

Contents

Preface

The purpose of *Reading Rousers* is to help you, the
teacher, to stimulate your students to read independently
through the use of a semiindividualized reading program.
Full-page activity sheets are provided which can be copied
directly and duplicated for use with individual students. To
assist you in organizing your reading program, the book is
divided into six sections:

MARVELOUS MAGIC (Modern Fantasy)
WAY BACK WHEN (Historical Fiction)
THINGS I WANT TO KNOW ABOUT (Informational Books)
HOW IT IS TODAY (Realistic Fiction)
THEY REALLY LIVED! (Biography)
ONCE UPON A TIME (Traditional Literature)

How to Use the Reading Rousers

Getting Ready

The first step in utilizing the Reading Rousers is to decide which of the activities are suitable for the students in your classroom.

NOTE: Many of these activity sheets may easily be adapted to various reading levels.

Once you have chosen the appropriate activity sheets, simply duplicate them so that you have enough for all the children in the class. If at all possible, these sheets should be run on paper of various colors in order to make them particularly appealing to the students.

Then, to assure that the students have easy access to the Reading Rousers, a dispenser

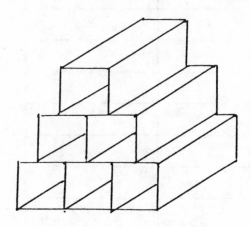

should be made. This can be done easily by cutting the tops off of six half-gallon milk cartons. Cover each of the milk cartons with bright contact paper and then, using tape or glue, attach these cartons together to form a pyramid, as shown. If a variety of Reading Rousers is placed in the containers, students will be able to browse and choose just the right one.

Introducing the Reading Rousers

Before the students begin to use the Reading Rousers in the dispenser, each of the activity sheets should be introduced to the class. Read the directions aloud and answer any questions that the students have. By doing this you will be saving yourself from many future questions.

IMPORTANT: Begin with only six Reading Rousers so that you can continually add new ones to spark interest. Then, as the variety of Reading Rousers increases, begin withdrawing some of the earlier sheets. (They may be used again at a later time.) By doing this you will be able to keep a freshness to the reading program.

Record Keeping

Once the children begin to use the Reading Rousers, you must have an easy-to-use and

READING ROUSERS
Student Record Form

Name _____

Date	Title	Subject	Evaluation	Comments

effective technique for keeping track of them. Two components can be made that are helpful here:

1. Make a deposit box for completed forms. This could be a cardboard box covered with contact paper. Be sure that the students understand that all completed Reading Rousers are to be filed in this container.
2. Duplicate the Reading Rousers Student Record Form so that you have one for every child in the class. Then, as you receive the reports, you can simply record the date, book title, subject area, and evaluation for each report on the appropriate form. You may want to use a simple evaluation system such as the following:

    + above average work
    ● average work
    − below average work

Space is also provided on the forms for jotting down other pertinent informa-tion, such as questions you may want to ask the child at a later date.

By keeping records of the children's independent reading habits, you will be able to offer individual suggestions for appropriate further reading. It is also possible to use the information to group those children who have read books about the same subject for a "Friday Interest Session." These are usually very popular and encourage discussion among the students.

Using the Bulletin Board

Interest is often stimulated in a variety of books when the Reading Rousers are used as part of an ever-changing bulletin board display. Children like to find out what other students in the class are reading, and to use the finished reports as a guide to what to read next. Some effective bulletin board displays are illustrated.

Books to go
Bananas over!

Can you guess who has been reading these Books

Stop CLOWNING around and read some of these books!

Book Prediction

You may want to use the following prediction activity sheets as an extra spark for encouraging your students to read. They are to be filled out by students prior to reading a book. A student should browse through a book, looking at pictures, the table of contents, chapter headings, etc., and, after this brief exposure, complete one of the activity sheets. When the student finishes reading the book, the activity sheet is reviewed in order to find out how accurate the predictions were.

You can construct a Time Machine such as that shown for storing these sheets. It can be made easily from a shoe box, wire coat hanger, and spools, and labeled with a felt-tipped pen.

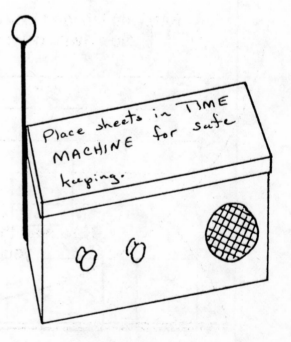

Place sheets in TIME MACHINE for safe keeping.

Look into the crystal ball

I think this book will be

_____ Make-believe   _____ About history

_____ An animal story   _____ A mystery

_____ A comedy   _____ About famous people

_____ Science fiction   _____ _____

I think the ending will be   I think the main character is

_____ Funny   _____ A Boy   _____ A girl

_____ Sad   _____ Nothing   _____ A machine

_____ Exciting   _____ A plant   _____ An animal

_____ Scary   _____ A building   _____ _____

_____ _____

Read the title and look at a few of the pictures in your book.
Now, what do you think the book will be about?

_____

_____

_____

_____

_____

Now read the book and see how good
your predictions are!!!

Book _____

Author _____

This card is from READING ROUSERS.   1980 Goodyear Publishing Company

Name _____

Date _____

I wonder
what this book
is about?

Draw a picture
of the main character.

How will you look when you finish this book? (circle one)

What do you think the book will be about?

_____
_____
_____
_____

Now read the book and see if you are right!

Book_____

Author _____

Name _____

Date _____

The Magic Pencil

Use your magic pencil and draw two things that you think will happen in this book.

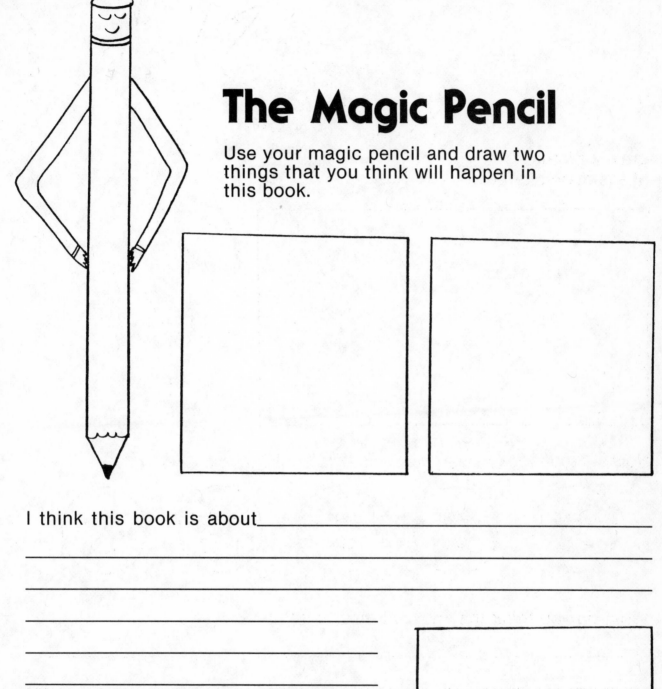

I think this book is about_____

_____

_____

Use your magic pencil again and draw how you think the story will end.

Book_____

Author _____

UNIT ONE

Marvelous Magic

MODERN FANTASY

Fantasy takes the reader into an unknown world or situation, populated with strange and unusual characters who seem very real. Books of fantasy hold a special appeal for children because the fantasy world created by an author is very much like the "half-real" world in which a child exists — where imagination flourishes and the impossible and improbable are seemingly accomplished.

The source of inspiration and the model for writing fantasy today is traditional folk literature. The true master and originator of modern fantasy is Hans Christian Andersen, who created beautiful and sensitively written stories that stated universal truths about mankind and often told of the sorrows and sadness of life. Many talented authors have followed him in writing fantasies that are allegorical in nature, containing a deeper meaning beyond the story line that relates to basic human characteristics and motives. A persistent and popular theme of fantasy chronicles the struggle between the forces of good and evil, that never-ending battle that concerns all of us.

Sometimes an author will develop a completely unreal world; other times, just a part of the world will be from the author's imagination, or the element of fantasy may be a magical power or magic object that a character possesses. However, no matter how the story develops, there are certain rules in the writing of fantasy that must be followed. The characters must be believable; they, themselves, must believe in the fantasy, and accept the extraordinary; and the fantasy part of the story must unfold in a logical and convincing way. Just as in any other type of story for children, the writing must be of the highest quality if the story is to hold a permanent place in children's affections.

There are several categories of writing that are found within the general classification of fantasy. These include humor; the personification of animals, toys or dolls, and mechanical objects; tall tales; and science fiction.

Humorous fantasy ranges in degree from hilarious slapstick to subtle, sophisticated whimsy and must be matched to the developing sense of humor of the child, or much of the enjoyment of the story will be lost. This kind of fantasy is very rewarding when shared in a classroom or home, for smiles and laughter are contagious, and increased enjoyment and understanding result.

It is very natural for children to accept stories in which animals, toys or dolls, or mechanical objects think, talk, act, and have feelings and emotions, for children often endow human qualities and characteristics to creatures and inanimate objects in their everyday world. These books are especially well liked by younger children, although they are appealing to all ages.

American tall tales comprise the only form of fantasy literature that originated within this country. These are the stories about the folk heroes of our country — Paul Bunyan, Mike Fink, and John Henry, among others — that describe in wondrous detail the exaggerated talents and capabilities of each. It seems that each section of our country has spawned its own particular legendary character.

Science fiction, in addition to meeting the general criteria for good writing, should also meet a special criterion: it must be based on a known scientific principle or speculative theory that could possibly be tested and proven at a later date. In fact, some science fiction written in the 1940s has actually happened to some degree in the 1960s and 1970s, notably in the area of space travel. Science fiction is not, however, confined to travel in space; it is often a projection into the world of the future of some current trend. Sometimes a book carries a warning that unless something is done to prevent it, a future disaster (such as air pollution to the point of complete atmospheric saturation) is not only

predictable, it is unavoidable. Some of the early science fiction books written for young children emphasized the humorous aspects of space travel rather than concentrating on scientific principles and thus have less appeal to the factual-minded child than those written recently. Science fiction, if well-written and credible, can combine science, mystery, adventure, and humor in an irresistible package that will provide absolute fascination for the reader.

For many years, the best written, most memorable fantasy was written by English authors, and even now English fantasy dominates the field. However, fantasy is universal and this field provides enough variety to offer something for nearly every reading taste, from the pure fun and excitement of tall tales to the deeper thinking engendered by the prophecies of science fiction.

Name _____

Date _____

Take a trip to the moon!

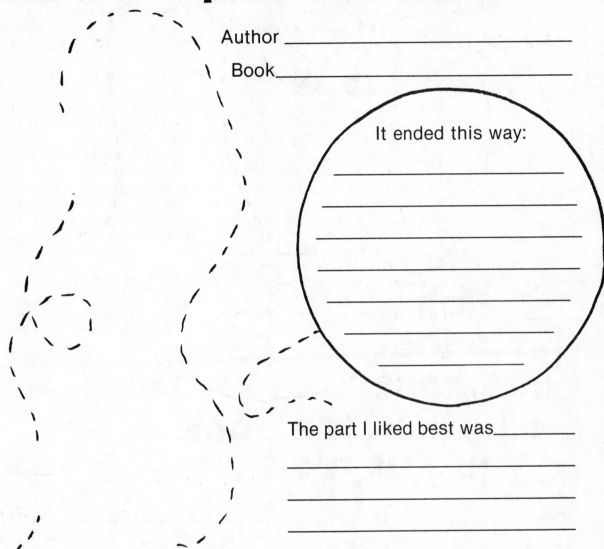

Author _____

Book _____

It ended this way:

_____
_____
_____
_____
_____
_____

The part I liked best was _____

_____
_____
_____
_____
_____
_____

Main Characters

_____
_____
_____
_____

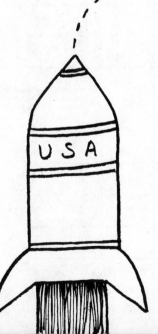

Tell Ernie the elephant all about the book you just read.

Book _____

Author _____

_____

_____

_____

_____

_____

_____

_____

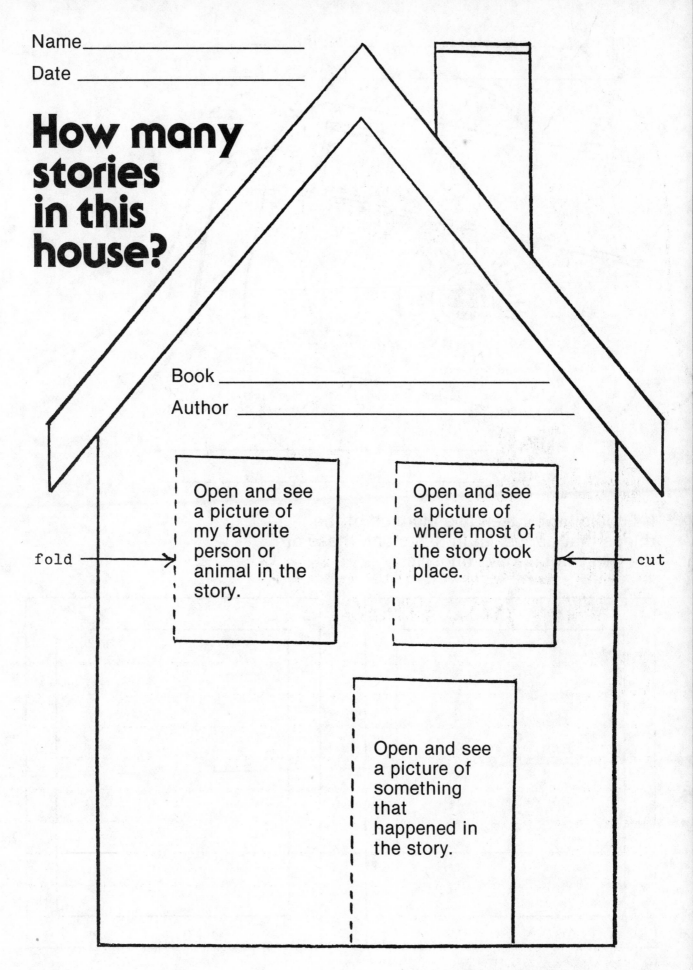

Name_____

Date _____

How many stories in this house?

This card is from READING ROUSERS. © 1980 Goodyear Publishing Company

Book _____

Author _____

fold →

Open and see a picture of my favorite person or animal in the story.

Open and see a picture of where most of the story took place.

← cut

Open and see a picture of something that happened in the story.

Name _____

Date _____

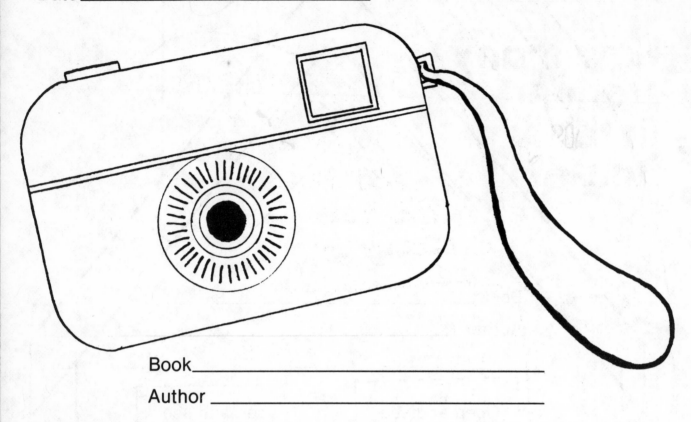

Book _____

Author _____

If I could have taken two pictures of the
things that happened in this story, these are
the two I would have chosen.

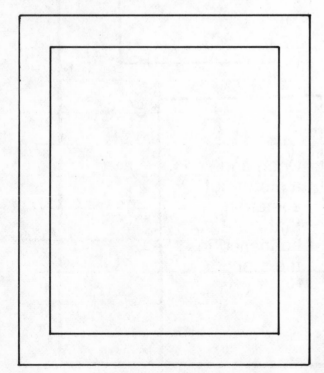 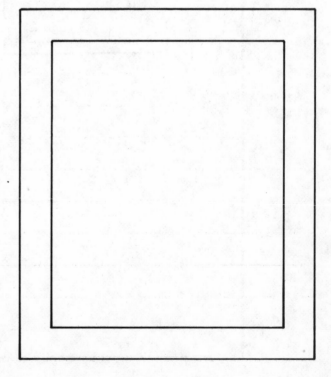

This card is from READING ROUSERS. © 1980 Goodyear Publishing Company

Name _____

Date _____

I'm going "BANANAS" over a book I just read! Let me tell you about it.

Book _____

Author _____

_____

_____

_____

_____

_____

_____

_____

_____

_____

_____

_____

_____

_____

_____

Name _____

Date _____

Magic Mirror

Look into this magic mirror and see a picture of my favorite scene from the book I have read.

Book _____

Author _____

Name _____

Date _____

I've just come back from a *strange land!!* The book I just finished took me to a land you've never heard of before. It is called_____.
Below is a map of the land. I'll show you where many of the things happened in the story.

Book_____

Author _____

- This is where_____
_____
_____
_____ .

- This is the place where
_____
_____
_____
_____ .

- _____
_____
_____
_____
happened here.

- It was here that_____
_____
_____
_____
_____
_____ .

Name _____

Date _____

If you want to take an exciting trip through space you
should read_____

_____

by _____

_____.

I really liked this book because_____

_____

_____. There were

lots of good parts, but the one I liked best was_____

_____.

If I could choose to be one of the characters in this story it would be___

_____

because_____

_____.

If I could actually do one of the things that happened in the story it would

be_____.

This card is from READING ROUSERS. 1980 Goodyear Publishing Company

Name _____

Date _____

The story I just read never could have really happened. It was make-believe! Here are some of the things that happened in the story that could not happen in real life.

Book_____

Author _____

_____

_____

_____

_____

_____

_____

_____

_____

_____

_____

This card is from READING ROUSERS. © 1980 Goodyear Publishing Company

UNIT 1/MARVELOUS MAGIC/Modern Fantasy **21**

Name _____

Date _____

Hi!

Book _____

Author _____

Hi! I just took two "make-you-invisible" pills and so now you can't see me. I took them because of the book I just read. Now that I'm invisible, I am going back into the story and help out _____, who was one of the main characters. By being invisible, I'll be able to trail this person and stop bad things from happening and sometimes make funny things happen.

The first thing I would do would be _____

_____

_____

_____

_____

Here are some other things I'd make happen.

_____

_____

_____

_____

_____

_____

_____

_____

This card is from READING ROUSERS. © 1980 Goodyear Publishing Company

Name _____

Date _____

Book _____

Author _____

I just read a story that was very scary!!
Let me tell you why it scared me. Here
are some of the scary parts.

_____

_____

_____

_____

_____

_____

_____

_____

_____

_____

_____

Name _____

Date _____

Magic Glasses

I have read about half of the book,_____,

by_____. These are a few of the things that

have happened so far:_____

_____

_____

_____

Now I have put on my magic glasses and looked into the future! What
do I think will happen as I read further into the story? I have chosen two
characters and written down what I think might happen to them.

_____

(first character)

_____

_____

_____

(second character)

_____

_____

This is how I think the story will end:_____

_____

This card is from READING ROUSERS. © 1980 Goodyear Publishing Company

Name _____

Date _____

Book _____

Author _____

Magic Carpet

Suppose I could ride this magic carpet back through the story I just read! There is one part where I would want it to stop so that I could really live it. I'll tell you all about it.

_____

_____

_____

_____

_____

_____

_____

_____

_____

Name _____

Date _____

I just read a book that I think is worth one thousand dollars!!!!! It's the best

book I've read in a long time. The title is_____

and the author is_____.

The story was about:

_____Strange lands   _____Animals

_____Toys or dolls   _____Magical powers

_____The supernatural   _____People who could do
                                            unusual things

The three things I liked best about this book are:

1. _____

_____

_____

2. _____

_____

_____

3. _____

_____

_____

This card is from READING ROUSERS.   1980 Goodyear Publishing Company

Name _____

Date _____

Bag of Gold

I just read a book that I think is worth a bag of gold! It's the best book I've read in a long time. The title is_____

_____

and the author is_____

_____.

The story was about_____

_____

_____

_____

The three things I liked best about this book are:

1. _____

_____

_____

2. _____

_____

_____

3. _____

_____

Name _____

Date _____

A Peach of a Book

I just read a peach of a book! That is, I really liked it and I'm going to read

another book by the same author. The book is called_____

and the author is_____

_____

It takes place_____

_____

_____

The main characters are_____

_____

_____

_____

The one I liked best was_____because_____

_____

_____

_____

One thing that happened in the book that I really liked was_____

_____

_____

_____

This card is from READING ROUSERS.   · 1980 Goodyear Publishing Company

Name _____

Date _____

Can You Guess?

I just finished reading a book and want to see if you can guess what it is about! I'll give you a clue by drawing something about it here.

Now can you guess? Well, here is one more clue.

The name of the book is_____and the

author is_____. It is about_____

_____

_____

_____

Name _____

Date _____

I dared to read this book.

Boy, don't read this book at night when you're alone! It just about scared

me to death! The title is_____

and it was written by_____. It is all about_____

_____

_____

_____

_____

_____

The scariest part of the story was when_____

_____

_____

_____

_____

I (was — was not) surprised at the ending because_____

_____

This card is from READING ROUSERS. © 1980 Goodyear Publishing Company

UNIT TWO

Way Back When

HISTORICAL FICTION

Nearly all young children have a curiosity about the past. "What happened when you were little?" and "What happened before I was born?" are questions that reveal this curiosity. At a simple level, these questions are asked of parents, grandparents, or other family members as children attempt to associate themselves in relationship to a world that once existed without them.

A rich and fascinating area of children's literature that satisfies this curiosity on a more extended and extensive level is that of historical fiction. Its richness stems from the fact that its origins are in the real historical past — people and events come to life once again for the reader. Its fascination lies in the recognition that others, regardless of their time or place, have experienced the same joys, uncertainties, emotions, thoughts, and hopes that we experience in our modern world. Historical fiction embodies the universality of human problems in an optimistic way, for it imparts the idea that somehow, in some way, humans have managed to survive even the worst of situations and have emerged with hope for the future.

In addition to meeting the primary requirement of good writing for children — an entertaining, interest-holding, absorbing plot — high quality historical fiction should also possess the added dimension of breathing life into history. A true and accurate retelling of what the past was really like will provide the reader with a deepened understanding of personalities and events that are sometimes described in a very sterile or necessarily limited manner in elementary-level textbooks. Authors of good historical fiction have to be sure that all details are accurately and authentically portrayed. Indeed, many authors research to such a great extent that more than one book results from the wealth of material they have uncovered. Many also become intrigued with a certain historical period and concentrate their writing therein.

A wealth of books concerned with American history is now available, with those about recent European history running a close second. All time periods have been covered, from the very beginnings of civilization in Africa and Asia to comparatively recent times.

Historical fiction can be used for a variety of purposes in the classroom, for it is a versatile tool. Not only can a teacher recommend one of these books for reading enjoyment, but certain books can also be correlated with studies in curricular areas as enrichment material. Such books have been written at all levels of difficulty, so in most instances, all the children in the class can find reading suitable for their level about the same time period. Thus all the children can contribute some information to a class discussion of the period under study. An added bonus is the attraction historical fiction has for many literal-minded children who may want to limit their reading to purely factual literature. Certain other skills also can be strengthened while using this kind of book. For example, maps can be made tracing pioneer or other routes, charts or graphs can be prepared of certain events or to show time lines, and geographical sites such as the rivers and mountain ranges mentioned in the stories can be learned.

From a teacher's practical viewpoint, historical fiction has many uses for imparting information; from a child's viewpoint, historical fiction tells a good story about the past. But no matter how historical fiction is viewed, or for what purpose it is read, it holds an appeal for all in its ageless timeliness!

Just picture that!

This card is from READING ROUSERS. ⓒ1980 Goodyear Publishing Company

Name _____

Date _____

Book _____

Author _____

Below in the picture frames are some of the things I remember best from this story.

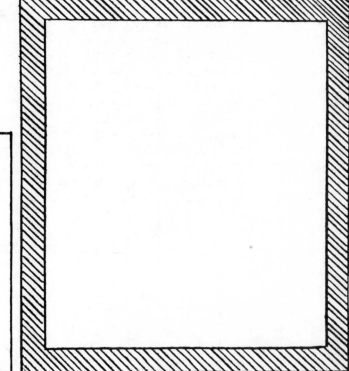

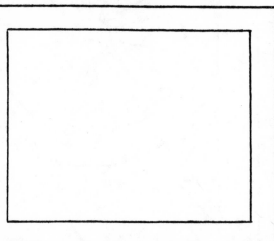

I think you (should — should not) read this story because _____

_____

_____ .

Name _____

Date _____

To while away the time
on long wagon train
drives, people used to
tell one another
stories. Tell part of the
story you just read.

Book _____

Author _____

UNIT 2/WAY BACK WHEN/Historical Fiction

This card is from READING ROUSERS. © 1980 Goodyear Publishing Company

Name _____

Date _____

Randolph Turtle can't read books but he loves to hear stories. Tell him all about the story you just finished reading.

Book_____

Author _____

_____

_____

_____

_____

_____

_____

_____

_____

_____

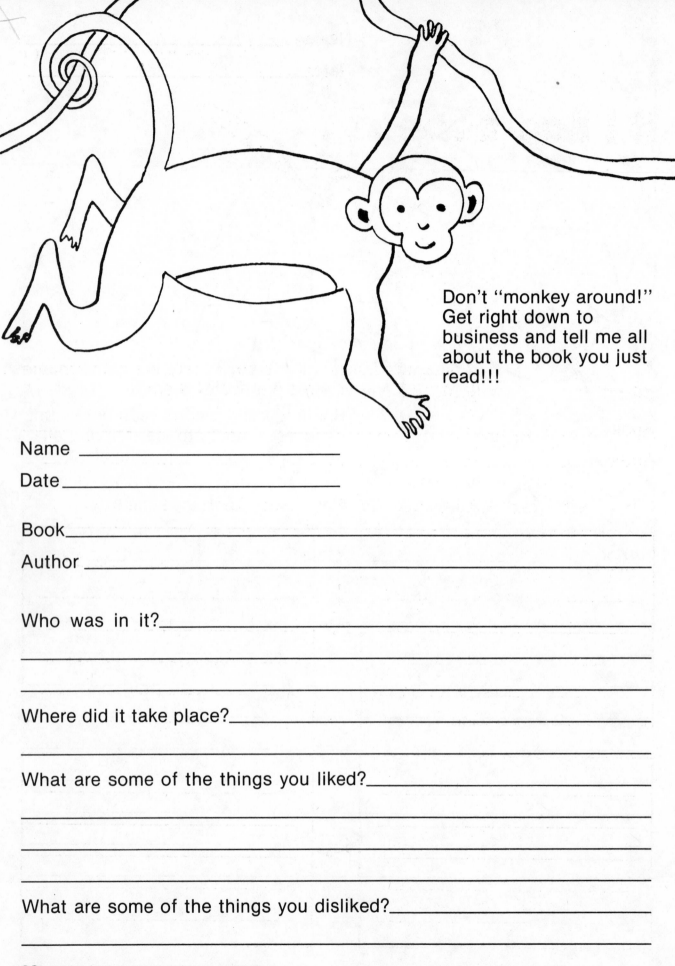

Don't "monkey around!"
Get right down to
business and tell me all
about the book you just
read!!!

Name _____

Date _____

Book _____

Author _____

Who was in it? _____

_____

_____

Where did it take place? _____

_____

What are some of the things you liked? _____

_____

_____

_____

What are some of the things you disliked? _____

_____

Name _____

Date _____

If I had been . . .

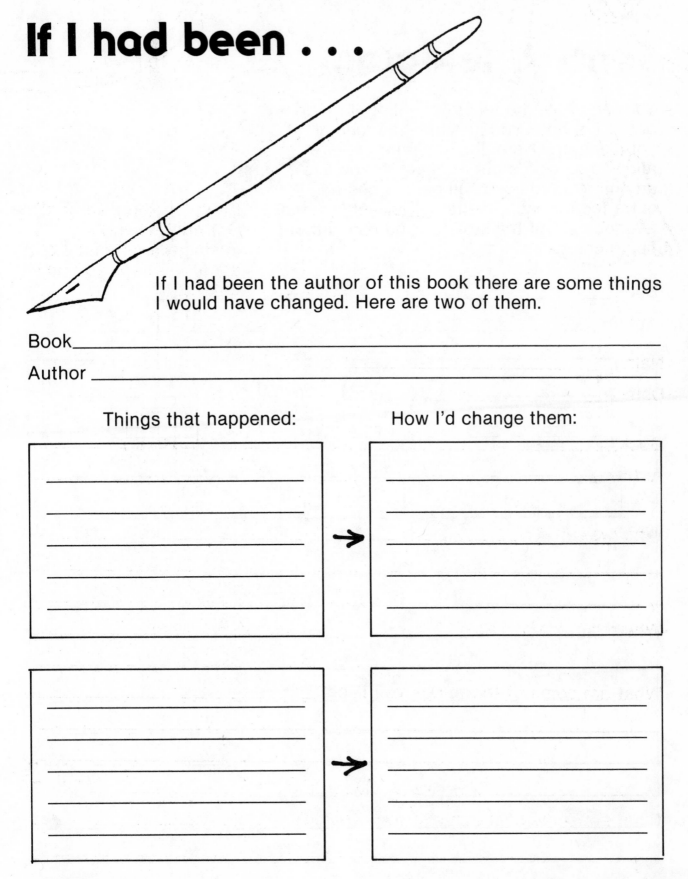

If I had been the author of this book there are some things I would have changed. Here are two of them.

Book _____

Author _____

Things that happened: How I'd change them:

$\rightarrow$

$\rightarrow$

Name _____

Date _____

Send A Telegram

You are to send a telegram telling a friend about the book you just finished reading. If you send an Overnight Telegram you are allowed 50 words but *no more*. If you use any more words you will be charged an extra fee for each additional one. Now send as much about the story as you can without being charged extra.

Book_____

Author _____

Western Union
Telegram

Yuk!!

I've just read the most AWFUL book in the world!!!

The title is_____

_____

and it was written by_____

_____

Don't ever read this book because _____

_____

_____

_____

The thing I especially did not like about this book is_____

_____

_____

_____

_____

These are several things that I would change if I could rewrite it:_____

_____

_____

Name _____

Date _____

I just read a firecracker of a book! Its title is_____

_____

It was written by_____

_____. I'll tell you the part I liked best, but I have to hurry before the firecracker EXPLODES!!!

Name _____

Date _____

Best Ever

Super

Great

Very Good

Good

Above Average

Average

Below Average

Bad

Awful

Worst Ever

How does it measure up?

I've just finished reading_____

_____

by _____

Using the scale on this sheet I would rate it

_____

This is because_____

_____

_____

_____

The thing I liked best about the story was

_____

_____

_____

_____

The thing I didn't like about the book was

_____

_____

_____

If I could have changed something in the

story, it would have been_____

_____

Name _____

Date _____

Time Line

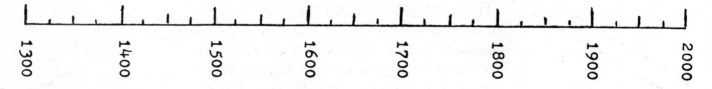

1300   1400   1500   1600   1700   1800   1900   2000

Place an "X" on the time line to
indicate when the story in your
book took place.

Book_____

Author _____

Where did the story take place?_____

_____

Who was the character you liked most?_____

Why? _____

_____

Who was the character you liked least?_____

_____

If you could change one thing in the story what would it be?_____

_____How would you

change it?_____

_____

I wish . . .

This story was about a family who lived long ago. A lot of nice things happened to this family but there were several things that I wish would not have happened. I've listed some of those bad things here.

Book _____

Author _____

1. _____
   _____

2. _____
   _____

3. _____
   _____

Name _____

Date _____

I just finished reading a
book about our early Americans.

It was about the _____

_____

Indians.

Book_____

Author_____

The thing I liked best was

_____

_____

_____

_____

_____

_____

The character I liked

best was_____

because _____

_____

_____

_____

Here is a drawing of
where he or she lived.

The thing I liked least was

_____

_____

_____

_____

_____

_____

This card is from READING ROUSERS. © 1980 Goodyear Publishing Company

Name _____

Date _____

I just turned back the hands of time and visited a part of our past. I did this by reading the book_____

_____

by _____

It was about_____

_____

_____

_____

_____

_____

It took place in_____

_____

I (would-wouldn't) have liked to live during this time because_____

_____

_____

_____

The thing I remember most about this story is_____

_____

_____

If I could change one thing about the story, it would be_____

_____

_____

I would rate this book as: (circle one)

EXCELLENT   VERY GOOD   GOOD   FAIR   POOR

Name _____

Date _____

Wow!

I just read a super book.

Book_____

Author _____

I really liked this book because_____

_____

_____

_____

_____

If I could choose to be one of the characters in this story, it would be_____

_____ because _____

_____

_____

_____

If I could actually live one of the things that happened in this story, it would

be_____

_____

_____

_____

Fly With Fred

Book _____

Author _____

Suppose you could climb on Fred's back and fly back through the story you just read. At which part would you want Fred to stop so you could really live it? Tell all about it.

_____

_____

_____

_____

_____

_____

_____

_____

_____

_____

_____

_____

_____

_____

Name _____

Date _____

Gee!

I just lassoed me a really good book, part-
ner! It was all about _____

_____

_____

I'll tell you about some of the things that happened!

_____

_____

_____

_____

_____

_____

_____

_____

_____

_____

_____

_____

Book _____

Author _____

This card is from READING ROUSERS. © 1980 Goodyear Publishing Company

Suppose you were walking down the street and met one of the main characters from the story you just finished reading. Not only that, but the person asked you several questions about the story. How would you answer them? Well try it!

Book_____

Author_____

Character_____

PARDON ME.... BUT AREN'T YOU_____?

"What did you like best of all the things that happened to me?"_____

_____

_____

_____

_____

"If you had been me, would you have done anything differently?"_____

_____

_____

_____

_____

"Who do you think my best friend is? Why?"_____

_____

_____

"If you could be one of my friends, which one would it be? Why?"_____

_____

_____

_____

_____

UNIT THREE

Things I Want to Know About

INFORMATIONAL BOOKS

Almost everything a child wants to know can be found in one of the numerous informational books that are available today. Many of these books are written with the style and grace that characterize the foremost fictional books for children, and they often combine information with humor while sparking the child's imaginative and creative qualities. Nonfiction books are no longer distinguished only for their usefulness, but also for their excellent literary quality.

The distinction between informational books and fiction is in their focus — informational books are primarily concerned with facts. This does not mean, however, that informational books cannot tell an interesting story, and many of them do. In some picture books for younger children, story and facts are often so successfully interwoven that it is difficult to determine the proper classification for the book. The accuracy of the facts is essential in a factual book, of course, but the book must also be well written to hold the attention and extend the interest of a curious child. Many adults find that the information given in children's books on certain topics is so clearly and thoroughly presented that they themselves need to do no further reading to possess an understanding of the topic. Nearly any area of factual

knowledge will catch and hold the interest of children (and adults) if it is written with good prose style and honesty of presentation. In fact, many children become so fascinated with these informative and exciting books, that they will read no others.

The organization and scope of these books varies, of course, in many ways, and for many reasons. If the intent of the author is to present general information about a broad topic, the organization will be considerably different than if the intent is to present limited information in depth. Some books presenting experiments contain a large amount of detailed instructions, while other books are purely descriptive.

Informational books are usually either written by an expert or well-known authority in some particular field, or by a writer who has an interest in a certain subject in consultation with experts. A careful and conscientious author will not allow personal opinions to color the factual material that is being presented, and also will bear the responsibility of showing both sides if two different beliefs about the subject exist. To be truly effective and helpful, an informational book should have a table of contents; an index; a glossary of difficult or technical terms; headings and subheadings; and drawings, diagrams, charts, or photographs that further enhance an understanding of the subject.

In addition to textbooks, many informational books have been written to correlate with the curricular areas taught in schools today. A book on any subject can usually be found for any grade level. A good author is very mindful of the capabilities and limitations of the intended audience, and strikes a delicate balance between simplification in terms a child can understand and the complexity needed for an accurate representation of the subject.

The biological sciences hold a lot of fascination for children, and books are available about plant and animal classification, genetics, ecology, relationships among living things, and the usefulness of plants used as food and fuel. There are books about one specific animal and survey books about many, identification books, and books on the cycles of plant and animal reproduction.

Books are also available that give detailed information about the physical sciences, including books about weather, rocketry, oceanography, astronomy, gravity, natural forces such as earthquakes and volcanoes, mathematical concepts, physics, chemistry, mechanics and energy, medicine, and electronics.

The social sciences, which give children a much clearer understanding of people and of the past, are abundantly represented on the bookshelves, including the areas of anthropology, history, political science, economics, geography, and law. Biographies of men and women who have contributed to the social development of the past and present fall into this category, as does one of the most popular types of nonfiction book — those that describe the settlement of America, bringing alive the spirit, hopes, and dreams of the people of other times.

Books about music, art, dance and architecture also have been written for children at various levels, as have books about various religions.

There are also many books in general interest areas, such as sports, crafts, photography, and pet care, which serve to broaden children's interests and extend talents. In addition, books utilizing the discovery method — including books on cooking — are found in abundance, either for generalized or specific subjects.

Whether it is used for a class project or to satisfy a child's own curiosity, a good informational book provides much more than just information. It provides stimulation and challenge and a constant fascination for an inquiring young mind.

Name _____

Date _____

The man-in-the-moon has been watching you read your book. He knows you liked it and wants to find out what it's about. Tell him about some of it!

Book _____

Author _____

_____

_____

_____

_____

_____

_____

_____

_____

_____

_____

_____

Name _____

Date _____

Facts, Facts, Facts!

I really learned a lot from this book I just finished reading. It was all about _____ _____ and here are some of the things I learned.

Book _____

Author _____

Name _____

Date _____

Book _____

Author _____

I just learned some things about a place I have never visited. If I could, I would actually travel there and see some of the things I learned about, including the following:

_____

_____

_____

_____

_____

_____

_____

_____

_____

_____

_____

_____

_____

_____

Name_____

Date _____

Book _____

Author _____

I just got back from someplace I'd never been before. This book I just

finished took me to_____

_____

Let me tell you about it. The thing I liked best about this place is_____

_____

_____

I (would — would not) want to live there because_____

_____

_____

_____

I learned some interesting things about this place. Here are a few you might

be interested in:_____

_____

_____

_____

_____

_____

This card is from READING ROUSERS. © 1980 Goodyear Publishing Company

Name _____

Date _____

Pretend you have just arrived home from spending two weeks in the country about which you have just read. Your friends and family meet you at the dock. Write down some of the things you'd tell them about the country!

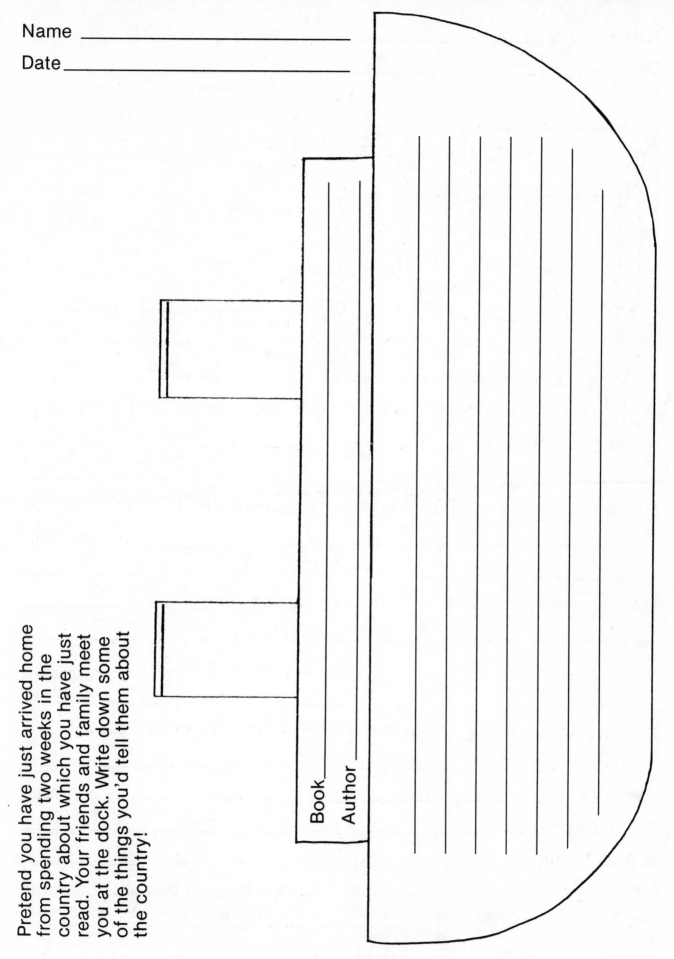

Book _____

Author _____

Name _____

Date _____

This card is from READING ROUSERS. © 1980 Goodyear Publishing Company

GLOBE

The book I read is about the_____War.

The title of the book is_____

and the author is_____.

If I had been a newspaper reporter then I would have written about several events. In fact, I've written about them in the newspaper on this sheet. (Be sure to give each article a heading!)

Name _____

Date _____

Billboards

These billboards advertise a city, state, or country
that I just read about. I hope they will make you want
to visit the place.

Book _____

Author _____

Name _____

Date _____

Time Machine

I have just been sent back in time through the use of a time machine.
When I arrived it was _____ in _____.
                                           (time)   (country)

I have been asked to write down all of the information I can for an
official report. Here are some of the things I'll never forget.

Official Report

Name _____

Date _____

Swimmy wants to learn about different things. He is interested in almost everything! So help him out; tell him about some of the things you just read about.

Book _____

Author _____

_____

_____

_____

_____

_____

_____

_____

_____

_____

_____

_____

_____

Name _____

Date _____

Happy Holiday!

I just finished a book about the _____
holiday. I learned some interesting facts about this holiday, two of which
are:

1. _____

_____

_____

_____

_____

_____

_____

_____

2. _____

_____

_____

_____

_____

_____

_____

_____

Here is a picture of something
that happens on this holiday. →

Book _____

Author _____

3

Name _____

Date _____

things I learned from the book_____

_____

by_____that   I

didn't know before I read it are:

1. _____

_____

_____

2. _____

_____

_____

3. _____

_____

_____

I (would-wouldn't) like to read other books about this subject because____

_____

_____

_____

_____

_____

Name _____

Date _____

The country I just read about in the

book_____

_____

by_____

is _____ .

Here are three things I learned about the country that I didn't know before I
read this book:

1. _____
_____
_____

2. _____
_____
_____

3. _____
_____
_____

One thing I didn't like about the book is_____
_____
_____

I (would-wouldn't) like to live in this country because_____
_____
_____

This card is from READING ROUSERS. © 1980 Goodyear Publishing Company

A Net Full of Reasons

Name _____

Date _____

I just finished reading

_____

_____ by _____

_____ .

Here is a net full of
reasons (to — not to)
read it!

_____

_____

_____

_____

_____

_____

_____

_____

_____

_____

_____

_____

_____

Name _____

Date _____

Help Henry!

Henry says, "I wish you'd tell me all about the book you just read, since I can't read!"

Book _____

Author _____

_____
_____
_____
_____
_____
_____
_____
_____
_____
_____
_____
_____
_____
_____

This card is from READING ROUSERS. © 1980 Goodyear Publishing Company

Name _____

Date _____

What makes it tick?

I've always wondered how a _____

_____works!

I found out all about it by reading a book called

_____.

It was written by _____.

Here is a diagram (picture) and a brief explanation
of how it works.

_____

_____

_____

_____

_____

_____

I (did — did not) find this book difficult to understand.

Name _____

Date _____

This was a most unusual book!

The name of this book is _____

_____ and it was

written by _____ .

The book was all about _____

_____

_____

_____

Here are five unusual things I found out by reading this book:

1. _____

_____

2. _____

_____

3. _____

_____

4. _____

_____

5. _____

_____

_____

I (do — do not) recommend this book to someone else.

This card is from READING ROUSERS. © 1980 Goodyear Publishing Company

UNIT FOUR

How It Is Today

REALISTIC FICTION

Realistic fiction first appeared in the middle of the nineteenth century and immediately became extremely popular with children and young people who felt a certain curiosity about themselves and their world. This popularity has now grown to the point where realistic novels almost dominate the field of writing for children. Contemporary realistic fiction discusses, in a frank and open manner, any and all topics that children can or may encounter in their daily lives.

Besides being extremely popular, realistic fiction is by far the most controversial of all of the types of literature written for children. The nature of some of the problems and situations described has necessitated a relaxation of some of the rules governing written language usage, as well as the inclusion of some unsavory details relating to certain life-styles. Controversy swirls around the extent to which this leniency should be permitted and whether it might have a harmful influence on the readers.

In order to qualify as realistic fiction a book must present a situation that could or did happen at one time or another, something "real." To qualify as *good* realistic fiction, the book also must meet certain other criteria, such as having convincing characterizations, an appropriate style, a credible plot, and a worthwhile theme.

While not all realistic novels are about problems or unpleasant situations in a child's life, many of them are. One of the most helpful aspects of realistic fiction lies in its ability to let children take an honest look at people and life as it is lived. They can recognize themselves, their friends, or their families, or they can read about life-styles or situations that are completely unfamiliar to them. This can give them an insight into the problems that others have that they never may have realized existed before. Realistic fiction clearly reflects our modern-day society with all of its complications and impossibly tangled relationships, as well as showing the joys and happiness that some people experience.

Children are usually concerned with their physical development which, in turn, affects their emotional development at every stage of their lives. They are concerned with what others think of them, worried about making friends and being popular, and of eventually achieving success in life. They are concerned about the proper societal ways of meeting their needs for receiving and giving love, and for belonging. Realistic fiction relates to all of these concerns.

A major focus of this type of fiction is, of

course, on the family. Stories of happy, well-adjusted families are plentiful, but they also honestly describe some of the everyday frictions of living together closely that prevent harmonious family relationships from existing all of the time. It is good for children to know that some of their strong, often hostile, feelings against another family member are natural and need not be a cause for guilty feelings. Reading about a happy family can give children an additional sense of security if they, too, are enclosed in loving relationships. Reading about such a family if it is different from their own can give children a glimpse into a more desirable world to be striven toward in later life.

Family problems, written about from the child's point of view, include those that arise from living in a one-parent home, a foster home, or a juvenile detention facility. Many books also have been written about divorce, illness and death, alcoholism, drug abuse, physical handicaps, mental illness, retardation, and any other type of problem that can and does exist. These books can help children by reassuring them that what they may be feeling or doing to cope in a similar situation is very normal, and by making them aware of circumstances under which friends or classmates live. Books on such subjects as drugs and alcohol can also serve, to some extent, a precautionary function.

Some of the many other subjects treated include old age and senility; the many forms of prejudice; finding the proper sexual role and dealing with and/or understanding deviant feelings in this regard; the many forms of violence — war and killing, murder, and the physical and mental crimes of rape and child abuse — and life in other lands and other cultures, including those outside of the religious, racial, and ethnic mainstream.

Other types of realistic fiction include animal stories, humorous stories, sports stories, and mysteries.

Most children feel a kind of bond between themselves and animals of every kind. They learn, early in life, to empathize with their pets, to give them love and receive an unquestioned devotion in return. Many animal stories, especially about horses and dogs, have been made into feature-length films or television specials, attesting to their continued popularity with children. Certain authors are especially well known for their ability to write about specific animals. Even though the major focus in a book may be on the animal, the child involved in the story generally undergoes some favorable developmental change due to his or her relationship with the animal in question.

Stories of humorous situations that are just plain fun are very good for children. In addition to helping to develop the reader's sense of humor, they also provide relaxation, enjoyment, and the chance to laugh at oneself as well as the characters in the book.

Both boys and girls are demanding more and more sports stories, not just factual information about the skills needed to participate in a sport, but stories about someone very actively involved, particularly a boy or girl. Unfortunately, very few good sports stories have been written at the primary level and there is only a slight increase in the number available at upper reading levels. A recent trend is to show the acceptance of a minority group member (including girls) or of a handicapped child as a worthwhile, contributing member of the team.

Mystery buffs can be of any age, and this is one form of realistic fiction that often remains a favorite throughout life. The challenge, adventure, and excitement of a well-written mystery keeps many a child up late at night, reading under the covers, just having to know how the story ends! Many excellent authors have devoted themselves to writing mysteries, but more are needed at the upper reading levels to offset the popularity of the predictable series' mysteries.

Realistic fiction is not only easy and fun to read; it holds out hope for the future and provides strength for meeting life as it is — good enough reasons for its continued popularity!

Name _____

Date _____

Send a Postcard

Now that you have finished reading a book, write a postcard to one of the characters you just read about. Tell him or her what you liked about the things he or she did. Write it as you would to a friend.

Book _____

Author _____

To:

Name _____

Date _____

See it on TV

This is the scene I would like to see on TV from the book I just read.

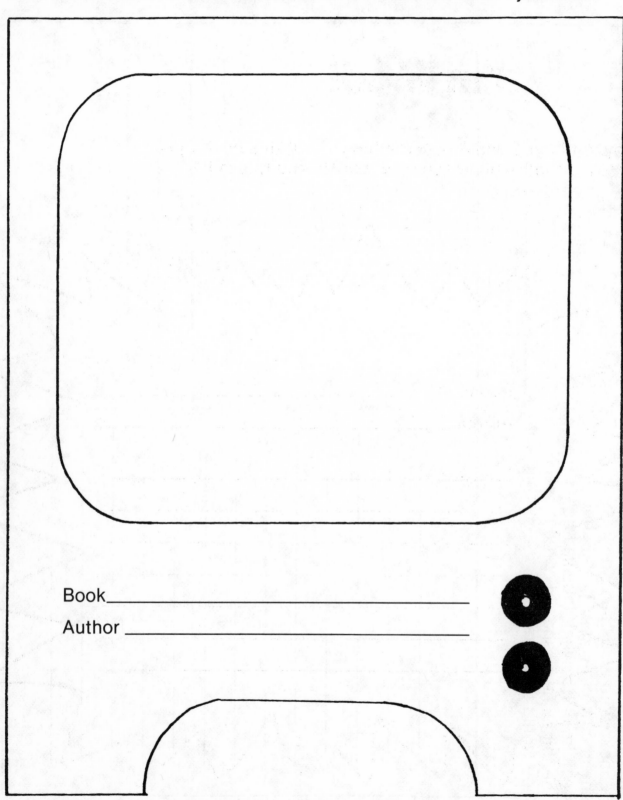

Book _____

Author _____

Name _____

Date _____

I'm Mad!

Boy, oh boy!!! There is something about this book I just finished that really makes me mad!!! And this is it!!

Book _____

Author _____

_____

_____

_____

_____

_____

_____

Name _____

Date _____

Ha Ha!

Ha Ha!

Hee Hee!

Haw Haw!

Ho Ho!

Har Har!

This book,_____

_____, was funny!

It was written by_____

This is one of the funniest things

that happened:

_____

_____

_____

_____

_____

_____

_____

_____

_____

_____

_____

This card is from READING ROUSERS.   1980 Goodyear Publishing Company

Name _____

Date _____

I just got hooked!

The book I just finished reading hooked me!!! That is, I really liked it and I'm going to read another book by the same author. The story is called

_____

and the author is_____

_____

It takes place in_____

_____

The main characters are_____

_____

_____

The one I liked best was_____

because _____

_____

_____

_____

One thing that happened in the story

that I really liked was_____

_____

_____

Name _____

Date _____

Touchdown!

Book _____

Author _____

If I could be a character in this story

it would be _____

because _____

One of the parts of this story I liked best was when _____

One of the parts of this story I liked least was when _____

The story ended like this: _____

This card is from READING ROUSERS. © 1980 Goodyear Publishing Company

One Strike

I just read a sports book about_____. The name

(sport)

of it is_____. The story was written by_____

_____. There (was — was not) enough sports action
in this book. The story (was — was not) very realistic when it came to
playing the games. I'll tell you a little about the book!

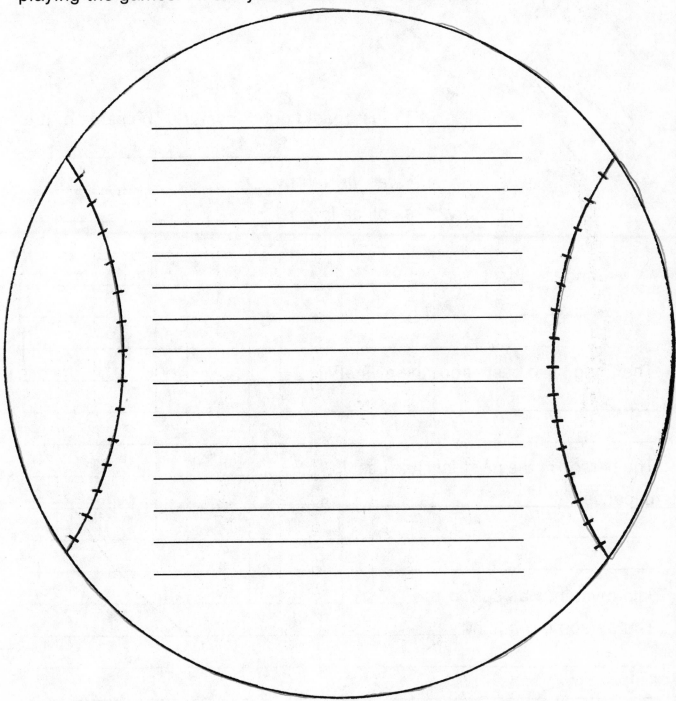

_____

_____

_____

_____

_____

_____

_____

_____

_____

_____

_____

_____

_____

_____

Name _____

Date _____

Wow!! I just read a good mystery. The name of it is

_____

and it was written by_____

The story takes place in_____

_____

and is about_____

_____

_____

The thing I like best about the mystery is_____

_____

_____

The person in the mystery I like best is_____

because _____

_____

_____

The mystery was solved by _____

The person did this by_____

_____

_____

This card is from READING ROUSERS. © 1980 Goodyear Publishing Company

Suppose you received a long distance telephone call from one of the main characters in the story you just finished reading. Not only that, but the character asked you several questions about the story. How would you answer them?

Book_____

Author _____

Character _____

"What did you like best of all the things that happened to me?"_____

_____

_____

_____

"If you had been me, would you have done anything differently?"_____

_____

_____

"Who do you think my best friend is? Why?"_____

_____

_____

"If you could be one of my friends, which one would you be? Why?"_____

_____

_____

Name _____

Date _____

There was something fishy about the book I just read. I thought it was going to be good, but it turned out to be boring. Here are the reasons why: _____

Book _____

Author _____

Name _____

Date _____

The Shadow!!

If you want to read a good mystery then

read_____

by_____

It takes place at_____

_____

_____ The main characters are _____

_____

_____

I don't want to spoil it for you so I won't tell you the

ending, but here is what the story is about:_____

_____

_____

_____

_____

_____

Name _____

Date _____

Dream On . . .

Book _____

Author _____

If I could be a character from this book it would

be _____

_____ because _____

_____

_____

_____

_____

But there are some things I'd change about this

person. They are _____

_____

_____

If I could actually live part of the story it would

be _____

_____

_____

_____

_____

This card is from READING ROUSERS. © 1980 Goodyear Publishing Company

Name _____

Date _____

Book _____

Author _____

You have just taped an interview with one of the characters from the book you have just finished reading. Tell us who this person is and write down some of his or her conversation. Don't forget to include the questions you asked!!!

Character _____

Interview

Question: _____

Answer: _____

_____

_____

Question: _____

Answer: _____

_____

_____

_____

Name _____

Date _____

I just read a honey of a book! The name of it is_____

_____. It was written by_____

_____. The reason I liked it was because_____

_____

_____

_____

_____

It was about:

_____Mystery   _____Animals

_____Sports   _____Children living in other countries

_____Children like me   _____Children with serious problems

If I could change one thing about the story it would be_____

_____

_____

_____

I (did — did not) like the ending because_____

_____

_____

_____

This card is from READING ROUSERS. © 1980 Goodyear Publishing Company

This card is from READING ROUSERS. © 1980 Goodyear Publishing Company

Name _____

Date _____

This book drove me CRAZY.

Book_____

Author _____

I liked part of this book but disliked others! I couldn't make up my mind whether I liked it or not! Help me to decide.

Here are two things I liked about it:

1. _____

   _____

2. _____

   _____

Here are two things I didn't like about it:

1. _____

   _____

2. _____

   _____

Well, what do you think, did I like it or not?

This is how the story ended:_____

_____

_____

_____

_____

_____

Name _____

Date _____

I just read a book that turned me on! The
title is _____

_____

_____and it was

written by_____

_____

The part I liked best was_____

_____

_____

_____

_____

_____

Three other things about the story that turned me on are:

1._____

_____

_____

_____

2._____

_____

_____

_____

3._____

_____

_____

_____

Open the Cupboard

This cupboard will tell you about the book I just read.

Book _____

Author _____

FOLD

Open and see a picture of my favorite person or animal in the story.

CUT

Open and see a picture of where most of the story took place.

Open and see a picture of something that happened in the story that I really liked.

Open and see a picture of something that happened in the story that I did not like.

UNIT FIVE

They Really Lived!

BIOGRAPHY

There is perhaps no other literature for young readers that is more inspirational than biography, for biography that is honestly written shows the humanness of the subject, offering a role model for children to emulate. Not all biographical subjects are necessarily famous men or women, for some significant figures quietly live to greatness without ever knowing public recognition. Biographies of unknown or lesser-known men and women show even more vividly the importance of caring for, helping, and respecting the rights of others — the hallmark of greatness, if not fame.

Children have a special appreciation for a story about a real person, and it is essential that this person be portrayed in as accurate a way as possible. Both good and not-so-good characteristics and qualities should be revealed to the reader, for if a young person tries to imitate someone who has seemingly never done anything wrong, never made any mistakes, he or she is attempting the impossible and will become frustrated and unhappy. However, biographers should apply the limits of good taste and discretion when writing for young people. Sordid details that add nothing to the life story are not mentioned because of young readers' inability to see the totality of the character if this kind of characteristic is presented.

A biography should also meet certain literary qualifications if it is to be of lasting value, and if it is to catch and hold the interest of children. The way in which the author puts together the facts and details of the subject's life is of the utmost importance. The mere accumulation of personal facts does not ensure an absorbing and exciting book. The author must use these details to impart a reality to the subject in a way that makes him or her live again for today's child. The style of writing is as important in a biography as in any other type of literature because it can improve the flow of the book. Illustrations, when appropriate, also add to the biography's realism.

Only a few autobiographies are available for children, although some have been written recently by sports figures. There are three basic types of biographies that figure importantly in children's literature today: authentic biography, fictionalized biography, and biographical fiction. All are popular, and all have distinguishing features as far as the treatment of the subject is concerned.

Authentic biography, as the name implies, is authentic down to the last detail. Only known statements made by the subject are included as dialogue in this kind of biography, and much careful research must be done to ensure the accuracy of the details. Authentic biographies for children are not as common as are the other two types.

Fictionalized biography is by far the most popular and most abundantly available type of biography written for children today. The characters and events in these books are authentic, having really existed and happened, but the author has invented dialogue and additional situations to give added interest and excitement to the story. Here again, the subject is carefully researched to provide accuracy of details, but the author is allowed a certain inventiveness as well.

Biographical fiction takes an actual character and weaves an imaginary story around this character; all the events and dialogue stem purely from the imagination of the author. The charm of this kind of biography — which is more fiction than biography — lies in the speculation that the imagined story might have really happened as the author has written it. Two notable examples of this kind of fiction are *Ben and Me*, a biography of Ben Franklin "written" by his mouse, Amos, and *Mr. Revere and I*, "written" by Paul Revere's horse. Both books are the creations of Robert Lawson, and both present a very interesting, though unorthodox, view of historical characters.

Another type of biography that is important in children's literature, and can be either authentic or fictionalized, is the partial biography, that takes a person to a certain point in his or her life and no further. This is often done in writing for children if unfortunate or tragic events not suitable for the intended age level are a part of the subject's life. At one time it was believed that children only were interested in reading about the childhood of famous people, but now it is acknowledged that the subject's entire life is of interest to a curious young reader.

Collective biographies also are available that focus on a group of people with a common occupation, profession, or dedication. Such books give brief, generalized biographical sketches of as many as twenty personalities. Readers may become so intrigued with one or more of these personalities that they then look for a biography that goes into greater depth.

Many of the biographies written for children are parts of series. One popular series is about famous adventurers and the discoveries they have made. Two series of "Beginning-to-Read" books portray the subjects as seen from a child's point of view. Another series focuses on biographies of minority group members. However, the excellence of each individual biography in any series is wholly dependent upon the talents of the author and should be judged alone.

Whether they are portrayed as accurately as possible or fictionalized, or whether they are described briefly, partially, or thoroughly, the lives of others always hold interest, and biographies hold a very important place in children's literature, today as always.

Famous People

I just read a book about_____
                                                    (person)

The title of the book is_____

and it was written by_____

I thought it (was — was not) a good book because_____

_____

_____

Here are some of the things I learned about this person:

_____

_____

_____

_____

_____

_____

_____

_____

_____

_____

I (would — would not) recommend this book to someone else.

Name _____

Date _____

Pocket Full!

This pocket belongs to_____.
(person)

It is stuffed with notes concerning an exciting life. (You are to fill in the notes that you think the person would have in the pocket!)

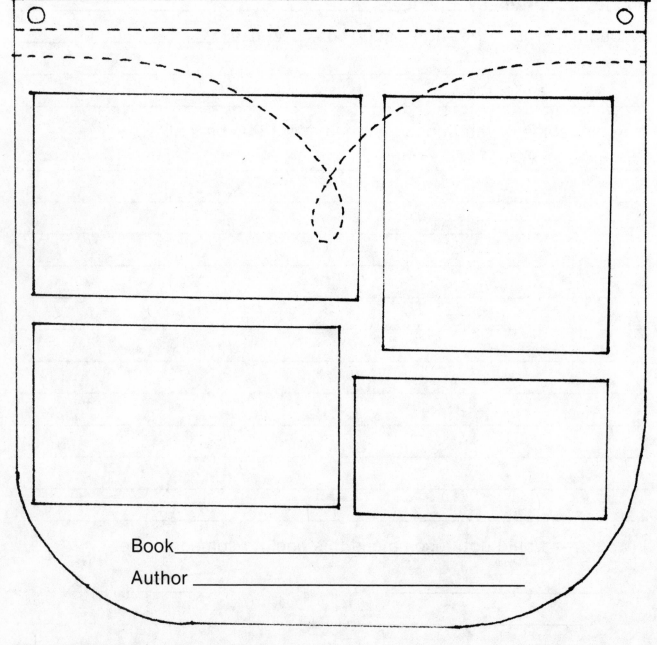

Book_____

Author _____

This card is from READING ROUSERS. © 1980 Goodyear Publishing Company

Name _____

Date _____

Family Tree

The family I just read about is very interesting. I will place some of the family members on the tree and tell something about each one.

Book_____

Author_____

Name _____

Date _____

Don't Be Nervous!

Gosh! You have just been chosen to interview_____
                                                          (person)
_____for a TV program. List below the questions
you would ask. Make sure the questions will draw responses about the
most important things that happened to this person.

1. _____

_____

_____

_____

2. _____

_____

_____

_____

3. _____

_____

_____

_____

4. _____

_____

_____

_____

Book_____

Author _____

Name _____

Date _____

Super Person

Wow!!!! I just read about a super person! I couldn't believe some of the things _____
(person)
did! Here are a few of them:

Book_____

Author _____

1. _____

_____

_____

2. _____

_____

_____

3. _____

_____

_____

Name _____

Date _____

Inventions Anyone?

I just read a book about_____.
                                                    (person)

The title of the book is_____and it was written

by_____. This person was an inventor.

Below I will draw one or two of the things they invented.

Someday I would like to invent something that would_____

_____. I would name it a

_____.

Name _____

Date _____

If this hat could talk, what a tale it could tell you! You see, it was worn by the very famous person I just read about. Oh, I know, let's pretend it *can* talk. This is probably what it would say about this person:

_____

_____

_____

_____

_____

_____

_____

_____

_____

_____

_____

_____

Book_____

Author_____

Name _____

Date _____

I just read about a famous scientist in the book

_____

by _____

The scientist's name is_____

The scientist is most famous for_____

_____

_____

Here are some things this person did:

1. _____

_____

_____

2. _____

_____

_____

3. _____

_____

_____

One of the most unusual things about this person's life is_____

_____

_____

The part of the book I liked best was_____

_____

_____

_____

_____

This card is from READING ROUSERS. © 1980 Goodyear Publishing Company

Name _____

Date _____

I am higher than a kite after reading about

_____,
(person)

who is one of the most amazing people I have
ever learned about.

I'm higher than a kite because_____

_____

_____

_____.

I read this in the book called_____

by _____.

Some of the things that amazed me about this
person are:_____

1. _____

_____

2. _____

_____

3. _____

_____

If I could relive part of this person's life, it would be when_____

_____

_____

Something I would not want to relive is_____

_____

This card is from READING ROUSERS. © 1980 Goodyear Publishing Company

If this desk could talk, it would tell
you about the person who used it. I
read about this person, in the book

_____

by _____ .

Now, pretend the desk really could talk. What would it tell us about the
person?

_____

_____

_____

_____

_____

_____

_____

_____

Name _____

Date _____

I just read a super book about a
super person in sports! This athlete's
name is _____.

This super-athlete is famous because

_____

_____

Here are some of the things this person accomplished:

_____

_____

_____

_____

_____

_____

_____

The thing that surprised me most about this person was_____

_____

_____

I (would-wouldn't) want to be this person's child because_____

_____

_____

Book_____

Author _____

Name _____

Date _____

Guess Who?

I just finished reading a book about a famous person.
I'll give you five facts about this person's life and
then see if you can guess who the person is. I will
write the names of the person, the book, and the
author on the back of this sheet.

1. _____

_____

_____

2. _____

_____

_____

3. _____

_____

_____

4. _____

_____

_____

5. _____

_____

_____

Do you think you know who the person is? Write the name here _____

_____Now turn over the sheet and see

if you guessed correctly!

Name _____

Date _____

I could
SCREAM!

I just read a book that really made me
mad!!! Let me tell you a little about the
story and why it made me so mad.

Book_____

Author _____

_____

_____

_____

_____

_____

_____

_____

_____

_____

_____

_____

Name _____

Date _____

What A Person!

I just read a book about_____.

(person)

The title of the book is_____and it was

written by_____ I thought it

(was — was not) a good book because_____

_____

_____

_____

Here are some of the things I learned about this person:

_____

_____

_____

_____

_____

_____

_____

_____

_____

_____

_____

_____

_____

I (would — would not) recommend this book to someone else.

UNIT SIX

Once Upon a Time
TRADITIONAL LITERATURE

Each country has a traditional or folk literature all its own, which originated orally and evolved and was refined by many different people. There are certain definite similarities among all of the stories, however, suggesting a bond of commonality in the values and customs of peoples everywhere. Such tales were used in the past, as much literature is used now, to instruct and teach morals and values, and to carry on the traditions of the individual cultures, as well as for entertainment. The happy endings of many of the stories satisfied a sense of justice; and the richness of glittering jewels, spacious castles, warm fires, and good and plentiful food reflected a common dream of having material needs satisfied. These storytellers, then, so important to their countrymen, wove tales that reinforced the hope for justice fairly done — evil punished and good rewarded — to those unfairly treated, and gave encouragement to young and old alike that dreams can come true. The various forms of traditional literature were the bonds that held societal forces intact, even furthering cultural values in a broad sense.

In today's world, when ethical values seem to be rejected by so many adults, it becomes extremely important that somehow, somewhere, children are exposed to the eternal truths about human characteristics. Traditional literature reveals that both bad and good are present in everyone, but the possibility of good winning out is exactly the inspiration children need to be encouraged to try to do their best. The encouragement of dreams is done just as effectively by this type of literature today as in years past; it still speaks hopefully of mankind to the children. The qualities of these old, well-loved stories still forge a link that strengthens an identification, a commonality of humanness, that gives dignity and worth to all peoples.

The traditional literature that is read by children today includes Mother Goose verses, ballads, folk tales, fables, myths, and epics and legends. While all of these different types of literature originated in the oral tradition, they did not all originate as stories designed especially for children. In fact, most of them were *not* designed for children at all, but were veiled, satirical comments on the conditions of contemporary society. The Mother Goose rhymes, for example, were thinly disguised criticisms of the rulers of the time. Scholars studying these verses can pin-point the majority of them in time and place as related to certain specific political personages. Because of their rhyme and rhythm, children, then as now, took them to heart and they have been their own ever since.

Children value ballads for the stories they tell, which take hold of the reader emotionally as the plot quickly and dramatically unfolds, often very tragically. The vigorous, lively refrains bring forth a bodily response that plunges a child into the midst of the story even more. Since ballads, like the Mother Goose verses, were sung originally for adults, they contain much violence, and should be carefully screened by a teacher before being used in the classroom to make sure that they are suitable for children.

Folk tales continue to be popular with children, perhaps more so than any other form of literature. Many theories exist about the origins of folk tales, but again, children appreciate the stories and don't wonder about how and where they originated. Older children may investigate sources as a class project, but the origin of a tale is of no importance otherwise, as far as the children are concerned. Younger children especially enjoy the cumulative tales because of their incremental verses and repetition, along with the talking-beast stories which often teach a lesson. Other types of folk tales include religious tales, humorous tales, stories with extraordinary personages (witches, giants, dwarfs, fairies, and anthropomorphic animals), stories of magic talents and magic objects, and stories of enchantments. All appeal to a child's imagination and, in addition, can be of great help in extending the child's understanding of human qualities, for every kind of emotion is explored in these old tales.

Fables teach a moral lesson in the briefest form possible, using few characters, and often have a written moral at the end. While these may not be as popular as other forms of folk literature with children because of their extreme briefness, fables still hold a place in the hearts of many. The recent, beautifully illustrated editions of single fables are held in high regard.

Myths are very fascinating to children, for they set forth what seems a logical explanation of certain natural phenomena in understandable terms. Even very young children can enjoy some of the simpler myths explaining the world's creation. However, the more complex myths about the lives and loves of various gods and goddesses must be carefully examined by the teacher for their suitability before being given to children to read.

Epics and legends both center around a national hero and his or her daring, though sometimes unsuccessful, exploits. Both types show the greatness of humankind, depicting the best and most admirable qualities that humans possess.

Traditional literature can greatly enhance and extend a child's understanding of self and others, and can be used advantageously in the classroom to clarify and strengthen the values of one's own culture and to instill an appreciation and respect for those whose heritage lies in a different culture. Beyond any applied uses, the stories provide entertainment and enjoyment as they reveal human relationships in an insightful way. Because of their continued popularity, many superb collections and single editions of traditional literary works are being issued and reissued to suit every taste. Traditional literature offers something for everyone!

Name _____

Date _____

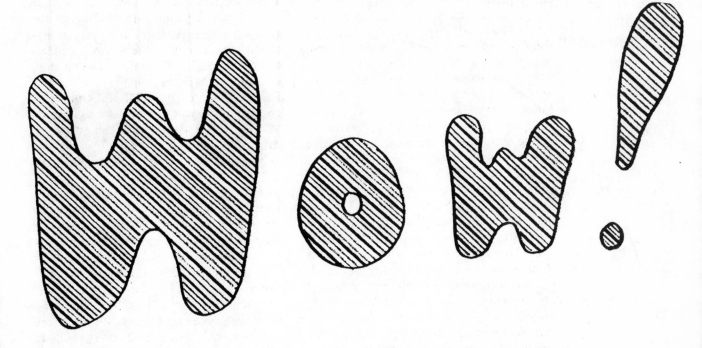

I just finished a super book. It's title is_____

_____ It was written by_____

The thing I liked most about it was_____

_____

_____

If I could change one thing about the story it would be_____

_____

_____

_____

It ended like this:_____

_____

_____

_____

Name _____

Date _____

See what I just finished
reading! I'll draw you one of my
favorite scenes.

Now I'll tell
you a little
about this scene.
_____

_____

_____

_____

Book_____

Author_____

This card is from READING ROUSERS. © 1980 Goodyear Publishing Company

A Bagful of Reasons . . .

I just finished reading_____by

_____. Here is a bagful of reasons (to — not to)

read it!

Name _____

Date _____

I just finished reading a book and want to see if you can guess what it is about! I'll give you a clue by drawing something about it in this circle.

Now can you guess? Well, here is one more clue.

The name of the book is_____

and the author is_____.

It is about_____.

Lucky Charm

This card is from READING ROUSERS. © 1980 Goodyear Publishing Company

Name _____

Date _____

Talk about being lucky!!! When I first saw this book I really didn't think I would like it, but I decided to try it anyway. Boy, am I glad I did! It is one of the best books I've ever read. It's about_____

_____.

I liked it because_____

_____

_____.

The part I liked best was_____

_____

_____. The character

I liked best was_____because _____

_____.

Book_____

Author _____

Name _____

Date _____

Stop!
Look!
Listen!

Stop, look, and listen while I tell you about the book I just read.

The title is _____

and it was written by _____

_____

The main characters are _____

_____

My favorite character in the story is _____

_____ because _____

_____

One of the things that happened that I liked best is _____

_____

If I could change one thing about the story it would be _____

_____

_____

I (liked — disliked) how the story ended because _____

_____

_____

This card is from READING ROUSERS. © 1980 Goodyear Publishing Company

This card is from READING ROUSERS. (c) 1980 Goodyear Publishing Company

Name _____

Date _____

WOW!

I just finished reading a very good adventure story!!!!! It was all about_____
_____

I'll tell you about some of the things that happened in the story:

Book_____

Author _____

Name _____

Date _____

Long before books were
developed, information
was written on scrolls.
Here is a drawing of a
scroll. Tell about the story
you just read by writing on
this scroll.

Book _____

Author _____

This card is from **READING ROUSERS**. © 1980 Goodyear Publishing Company

114 UNIT 6/ONCE UPON A TIME/Traditional Literature

This card is from READING ROUSERS. © 1980 Goodyear Publishing Company

Name _____

Date _____

The story I just read took place back in the days when most people lived in and around castles.

My favorite part of the story was_____

_____

_____

_____

_____

_____

I (would — wouldn't) have wanted to live during this time because_____

_____

_____

_____

_____

The character I disliked most was_____

because _____

_____

_____

This is how the story ended:_____

_____

_____

_____

Book_____

Author _____

Name _____

Date _____

Behind this door lurks a fabulous mystery!!!

I just read about it in_____

_____

by_____ .

The story began when_____

_____

_____

_____

_____

One of my favorite parts of the story was when_____

_____

_____

_____

_____The character I disliked most in the story was_____

because _____

_____

The thing that surprised me most about this story was_____

_____

_____

_____

I (did — didn't) think the story would end the way it did.

This card is from READING ROUSERS. © 1980 Goodyear Publishing Company

This card is from READING ROUSERS. © 1980 Goodyear Publishing Company

Name _____

Date _____

Help our spider to spin a tale!
Choose your favorite part of the
book you just read and tell about it.
Write on the web below, starting in
the center and working your way
out to the edge. You will have to
keep turning this sheet in order to
do this! Now don't get dizzy!!!

Book_____

Author _____

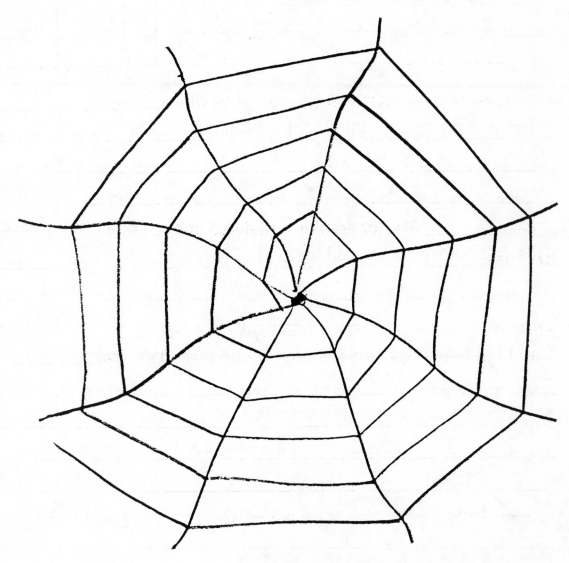

Name _____

Date _____

Even the Abominable Snowman
would like this book!

Book _____

Author _____

The thing I liked best about this book
was _____
_____
_____
_____
_____
_____

If I could change one thing in this book, it would be _____
_____
_____
_____

This is how the story ended: _____
_____
_____
_____
_____

My favorite character in the story is _____
_____ because _____
_____
_____
_____

This card is from READING ROUSERS. · 1980 Goodyear Publishing Company

Name _____

Date _____

I really dig this book I just finished!

The name of the book is_____

_____

and it was written by_____

_____

The thing I liked most about this

book was _____

_____

_____

_____

The main character in this book is_____.

If I could relive something that happened to this character it would be___

_____

_____

_____

_____

_____

If I could change something that happened to this character it would be___

_____

_____

My least favorite character in this book is_____

because _____

_____

_____

Name _____

Date _____

Wow!! This book hit me like
a bolt of lightning!!! The
title of the book was _____
_____
and it was written by _____
_____
_____

Here are three of the things that
really made me like this book:

1. _____
_____
_____
_____

2. _____
_____
_____
_____

3. _____
_____
_____
_____

This card is from READING ROUSERS. © 1980 Goodyear Publishing Company

Up in the Clouds

I'm up in the clouds after reading

_____

_____

by_____

_____

If I could be a character in
this story it would be_____
_____because _____
_____
_____

One of the parts I liked best was when_____
_____
_____
_____
_____

One of the parts of this story I liked least was when_____
_____
_____
_____
_____

The story ended like this:_____
_____
_____
_____

Name _____

Date _____

If I could . . .

If I could be a character from the book I just read it

would be _____

because _____

_____

_____

_____

But there are some things I'd change about this person.

They are _____

_____

_____

_____

_____

_____

If I could actually live part of the story it would be_____

_____

_____

_____

_____

_____

_____

_____

Book_____

Author _____

This card is from READING ROUSERS. © 1980 Goodyear Publishing Company